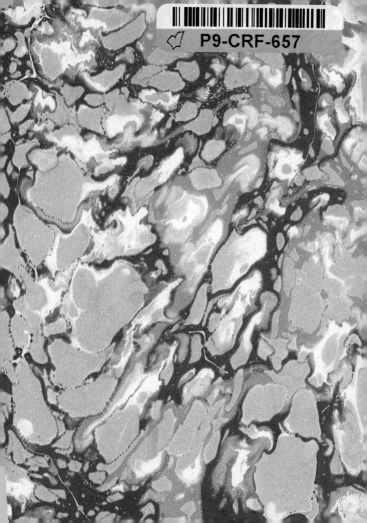

LOVING THOUGHTS
for
A Perfect Day

Louise L. Hay

Hay House
Carson, California

Library of Congress Cataloging-in-Publication Data

Hay, Louise L.
    Loving thoughts for a perfect day / Louise L. Hay.
       p.   cm.
    ISBN 1-56170-069-X : $5.95
    1. Affirmations. 2. Attitude (Psychology) 3. Self-actualization (Psychology) I. Title.
BF697.5.S47H39 1993
158'.12--dc20   93-13178
                                                 CIP

Design & Typesetting by: Michele Lanci-Altomare

93 94 95 96 97 98   10 9 8 7 6 5 4 3 2 1
First Printing, September 1993

Published and Distributed in the United States by:
Hay House, Inc.
P.O. Box 6204
Carson, CA 90749-6204

Printed in the United States of America
on Recycled Paper

INTRODUCTION

The power of positive thinking is a well-known healing force even within the medical community. The positive, loving thoughts on the following pages are nothing more than positive affirmations.

You may feel that thinking a positive thought cannot possibly change your life, but how many times have you repeatedly affirmed a negative thought about yourself until finally it became true for you? Why not change those negative thoughts to positive ones?

I like to compare positive affirmations to planting a seed. You don't just plant the seed and get a beautiful flower the next day. It takes time. First you must water and nurture the seed and make sure it is safe from harm. It is the same with positive affirmations. You may not see changes immediately, but with enough nurturing and encouragement you can change your old negative way of thinking and look at things in a new and positive light.

Use these affirmations daily and over time you will begin to see your life turn in new direction and you will reap a bountiful harvest of positive, loving endeavors for yourself.

All is well,

Louise L. Hay

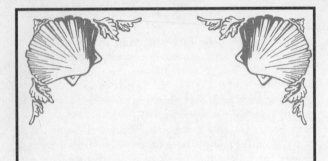

Today...

*begins
with gratitude
and joy.*

Today...

*I open
a new door
of understanding.*

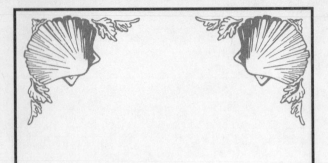

Today...

I am
willing to let go of
all negative beliefs
and to allow my own
deeper wisdom
to reveal itself
to me.

Today....

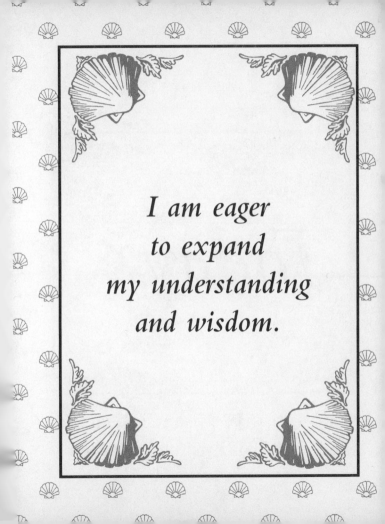

*I am eager
to expand
my understanding
and wisdom.*

Today...

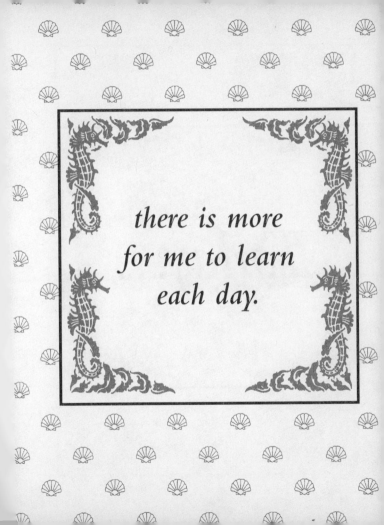

there is more
for me to learn
each day.

Today...

*I choose thoughts
that support
and nourish me.*

Today...

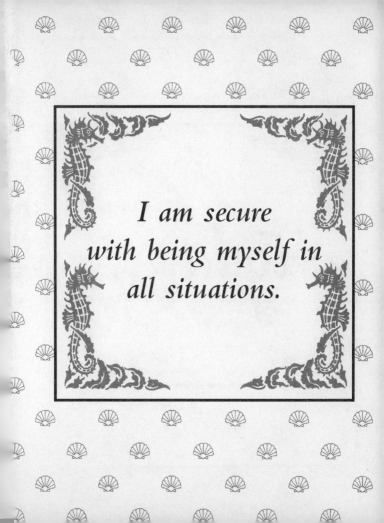

I am secure with being myself in all situations.

Today...

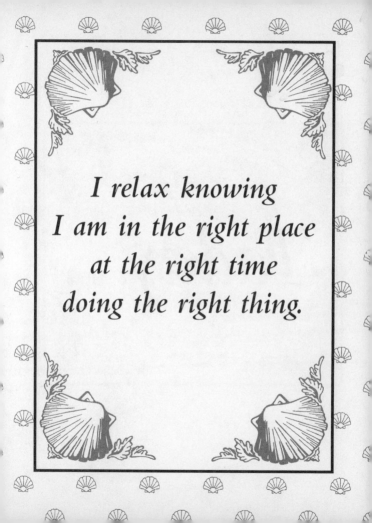

*I relax knowing
I am in the right place
at the right time
doing the right thing.*

Today...

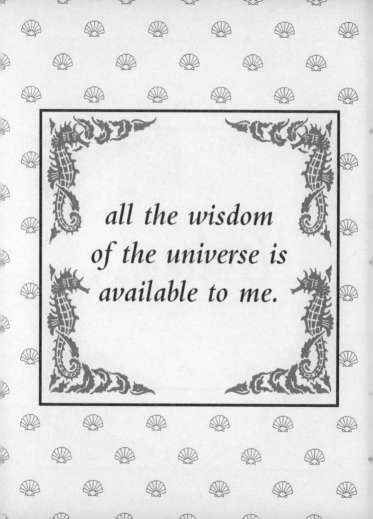

all the wisdom of the universe is available to me.

Today...

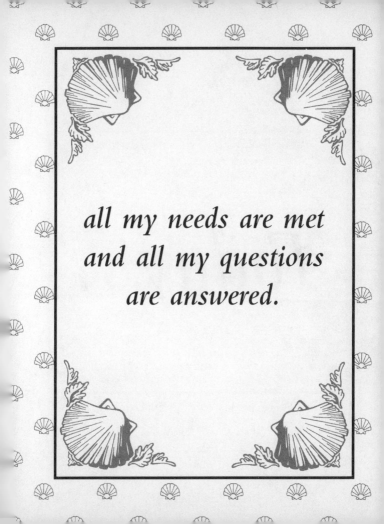

all my needs are met and all my questions are answered.

Today...

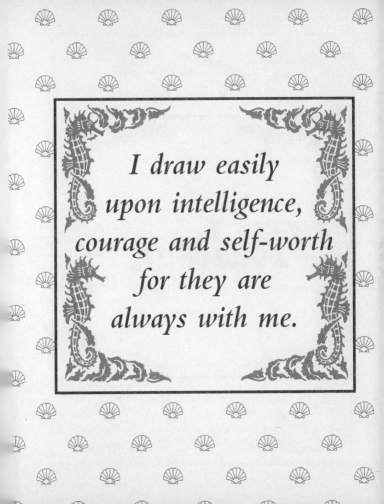

I draw easily upon intelligence, courage and self-worth for they are always with me.

Today...

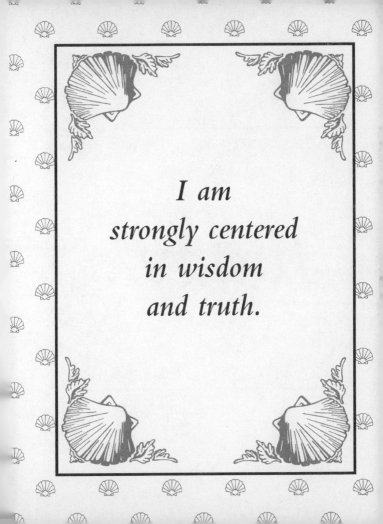

*I am
strongly centered
in wisdom
and truth.*

Today...

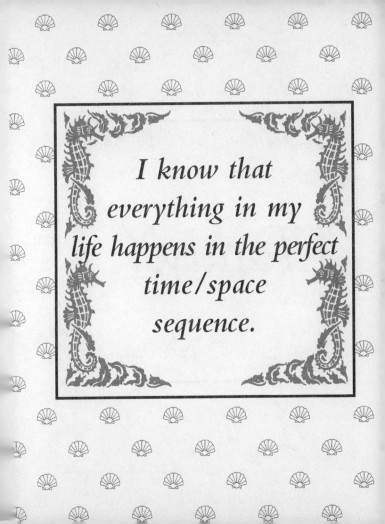

I know that everything in my life happens in the perfect time/space sequence.

Today...

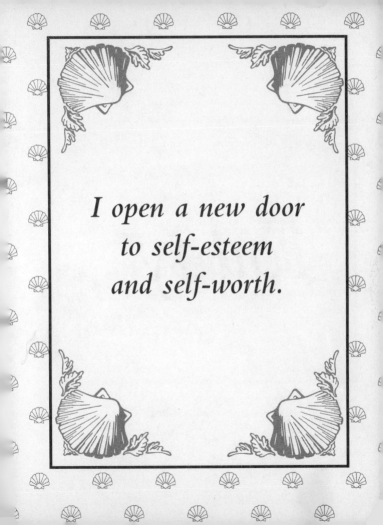

*I open a new door
to self-esteem
and self-worth.*

Today...

my life
is
getting better.

Today...

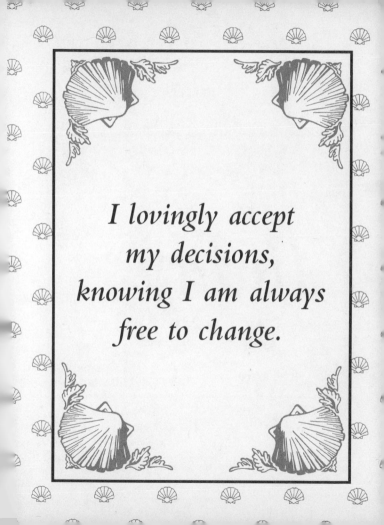

*I lovingly accept
my decisions,
knowing I am always
free to change.*

Today...

*I move forward
with confidence
and ease.*

Today...

*I rely on
Divine Wisdom
and Guidance
to protect me.*

Today…

*when I listen to
my inner self
I hear
the answers
I need.*

Today...

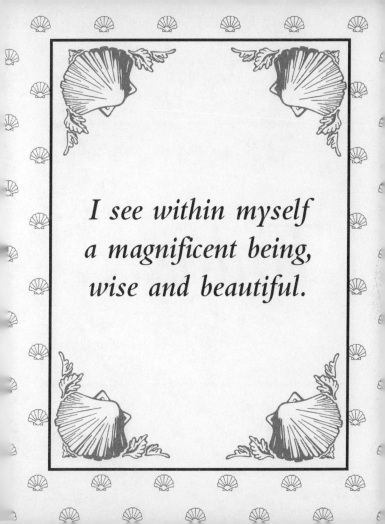

*I see within myself
a magnificent being,
wise and beautiful.*

Today...

whatever
I need to know
is revealed
to me.

Today...

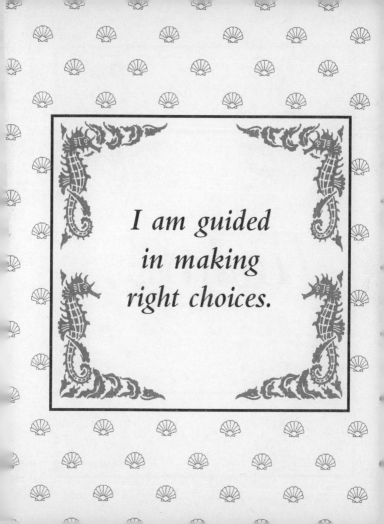

*I am guided
in making
right choices.*

Today...

*I release the need
to blame anyone,
including myself.*

Today...

*habits and beliefs
that are no longer
for my highest good
fall away from me.*

Today...

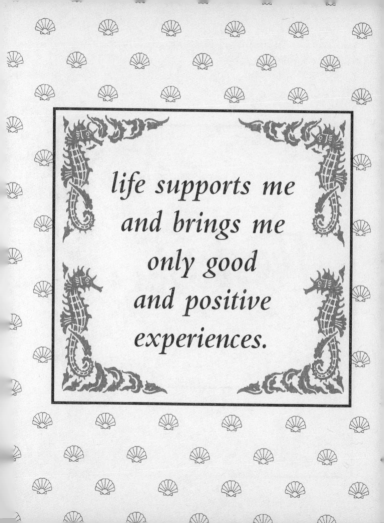

life supports me and brings me only good and positive experiences.

Today...

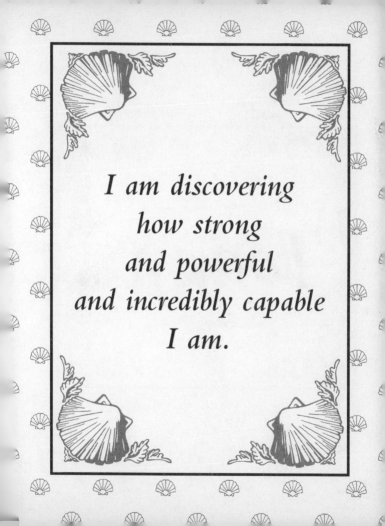

*I am discovering
how strong
and powerful
and incredibly capable
I am.*

Today...

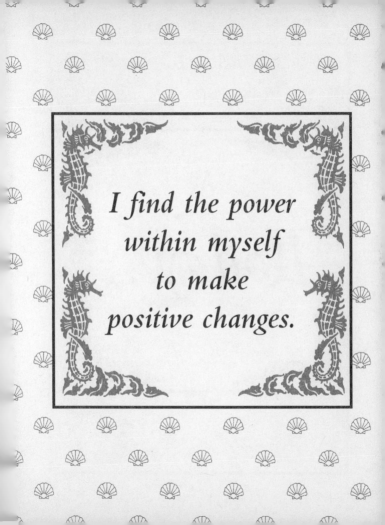

I find the power within myself to make positive changes.

Today...

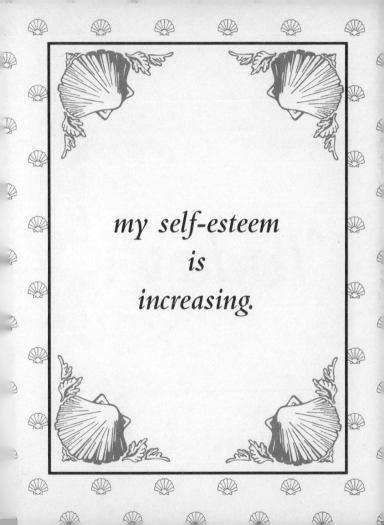

*my self-esteem
is
increasing.*

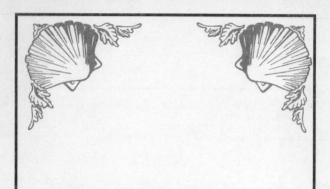

Today...

*I know
life is for me
and I joyfully
look forward
to the future.*

Today...

all is well
in my
loving world.

BOOKS IN THIS SERIES

Loving Thoughts for a Perfect Day
Loving Thoughts for Health and Healing
Loving Thoughts for Increasing Prosperity
Loving Thoughts for Loving Yourself

For a free catalog, call
1-800-654-5126